# 1001 Ways to Celebrate America

by Gregory J. P. Godek
and
Antoinette Kuritz

**TRIUMPH**
B O O K S
CHICAGO

This book is available in quantity at special discounts for your group or organization. For further information, contact:

Triumph Books
601 South LaSalle Street
Suite 500
Chicago, Illinois 60605
(312) 939-3330
Fax (312) 663-3557

Printed in the United States of America.

ISBN 1-57243-467-8

Cover design by Eileen Wagner.
Book design by Patricia Frey.

# Dedications

To the rescue workers and the survivors and victims of September 11, 2001 and the example you have set for the children—the future of America, the hope of the world.

*To Lieutenant John Godek USN—, my Dad.*

—Greg

*To my family, Rich, Marc, Alyscia and Jake—your love and support inspire me to be my better self. And to Zak and Aurora, who embody the best of the American Spirit.*

—Antoinette

*Special thanks to Nichole Mann. You rock!*

# About the Authors

Gregory J.P. Godek is best known for his massive best-seller *1001 Ways To Be Romantic* and for his outrageous relationship seminars. His personal and professional lives have always been about love. This new book is a natural extension, as it's about love of country, and connections to the people we love. Greg has discussed love on *Oprah* and counseled the "romantically impaired" on Donahue; he has been featured in *The New York Times* and quoted in *People* magazine.

Antoinette Kuritz is a literary publicist and writer who has represented clients as diverse as psychic medium John Edward, 1999 International Reading Association Award winner John H. Ritter, and *Rain Of Gold* author Victor Villasenor. She is also featured in *Chicken Soup for the Mother's Soul*. A former teacher and a Mom, Antoinette believes that we should remind ourselves regularly just how lucky we are to be Americans—and of the responsibility that goes with that privilege.

# ★ Introduction

Of all the places we could have been born in this world, of all the countries we could choose to make our own, we are lucky to be here—in the United States of America! We are a nation made up primarily of immigrants, of spirited adventurers intent on finding a better life in a better place. That is our history and our legacy, and our past, present and future strength.

We are and we continue to be the land of the free, the home of the brave. Although that distinction has sometimes made us complacent, it has also made us among the most generous and caring people in the world. Food grown by our farmers is distributed around the world. American troops are sent abroad to ensure the maintenance of human rights. American citizens are depended on to provide protection and sustenance. Being an innovative, successful, philanthropic, and diverse nation, we have a lot to celebrate—tenacity, perseverance, ingenuity, generosity, spirit, creativity, and so much more.

*1001 Ways to Celebrate America* is a reflection on two questions.

- ■ Just what is it that makes America America? What combination of people, events, places, achievements, statements and values makes us who we are?
- ■ What can we do to express our love of country, our unique character?

Turning to family, friends, and others for ideas, we have compiled a list of 1001 Ways to Celebrate America. You may agree with some, disagree with others, and want to add some of your own. We invite you to personalize your copy of the book by writing your own ideas in it and to share your suggestions with us by mailing us at P.O. Box 178122; San Diego, CA 92177.

Celebrate being an American. Celebrate well and often. Recognize it for the gift it is!

—Greg and Antoinette

Celebrate our unity.

Honor our diversity.

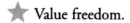 Value freedom.

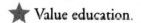 Value education.

Value creativity.

Value change.

Value inclusion.

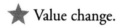 Value innovation.

Value ingenuity.

 Use your freedom to access education so that you can access your creativity and ingenuity.

Accept that inclusion promotes healthy growth and change, which lead to innovation.

# Identify these phrases:

"Four score and seven years ago…"

"Frankly, my dear, I don't give a damn."

"Here's looking at you, kid."

"And that's the way it is…"

"Live long and prosper."

"Is that your final answer?"

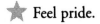 Feel pride.

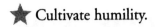 Cultivate humility.

Practice forgiveness.

Learn compromise.

Foster understanding.

Teach tolerance.

Develop patience.

Visualize peace.

# *Celebrate joyous holiday traditions . . .*

Rattle a noisemaker at the dawn of the New Year.

Leave cookies and milk for Santa.

Light Chanukah candles as a family.

Make a wish on the wishbone at Thanksgiving.

Color eggs at Easter.

Drink green beer on St. Patrick's Day.

# ⭐ Recall these great American images:

The Statue of Liberty.

The Empire State Building.

The "HOLLYWOOD" sign in Los Angeles.

The driving of the golden spike at the completion of the transcontinental railroad.

The Apollo spacecraft taking off.

"The Four Freedoms," by Norman Rockwell.

Hug your wife or husband;
boyfriend or girlfriend.

 Hug your Mom.

 Hug your Dad.

 Hug your kids.

Hug your pets.

 Hug your friends.

 Oh, heck—go hug a stranger!

## On Monday . . .

Be patriotic.

## On Tuesday . . .

Be efficient.

## On Wednesday . . .

Be happy.

## On Thursday . . .

Be creative.

## On Friday . . .

Be friendly.

## On Saturday . . .

Be with your family.

## On Sunday . . .

Be thankful.

# Read a great American novel:

*The Last of the Mohicans*, James Fenimore Cooper.

*The Scarlet Letter*, by Nathaniel Hawthorne.

*Moby Dick*, by Herman Melville.

*A Connecticut Yankee in King Arthur's Court*, by Mark Twain.

*Sister Carrie*, by Theodore Dreiser.

*The House of Mirth*, by Edith Wharton.

*The Jungle*, by Upton Sinclair.

*The Great Gatsby*, by F. Scott Fitzgerald.

*The Grapes of Wrath*, by John Steinbeck.

*For Whom the Bell Tolls*, by Ernest Hemingway.

*The Catcher in the Rye*, by J.D. Salinger.

*Catch 22*, by Joseph Heller.

# Explore the wonders of our United States . . .

Visit the Grand Canyon.

Take a picture of Mount Rushmore.

Climb a part of Pike's Peak.

Plant a sequoia seed.

Take a cruise on the Potomac River.

Cross the Golden Gate Bridge.

Visit Plymouth Rock.

Walk Navy Pier in Chicago.

Have dinner in the Space Needle in Seattle.

Drive past the Arch in St. Louis.

Drive through Death Valley (bring lots of water).

Drive historic Route 66.

Play Monopoly.

 Play the game of Life.

 Play chess.

Play Scrabble.

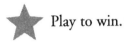 Play to win.

 Be a graceful loser.

# ⭐ Bigger than life:

John Wayne.

Superman.

Abraham Lincoln.

Captain Ahab.

Ernest Hemingway.

Marilyn Monroe.

Mae West.

Bake Toll House cookies.

 Eat them while they're hot.

 Dunk them in ice cold milk.

 Share them with family and friends.

Be thankful for the democratic process of our republic.

 Understand our political process.

 Understand the three branches of our national government.

 Understand the system of checks and balances.

Participate in jury duty.

 Learn the names of your local elected officials.

 Learn the names of your national elected officials.

 Obey the laws of our land.

# Great American Achievements:

Landing a man on the moon.

Voting rights for all citizens.

The Declaration of Independence.

The U.S. Constitution.

The Bill of Rights.

The U.S. Postal Service.

The public library system.

The Allied victory in World War II.

The separation of church and state.

Peaceful transfer of power following all elections.

Satellite communications.

Visit Ellis Island.

 Study Ellis Island records for the names of your ancestors.

 Get photocopies of documents from Ellis Island.

 Share the copies with family members.

 Compare the country of your family's origin to America to gain a better understanding of why your ancestors immigrated.

Gather your family photos.

 Interview your grandparents and great-grandparents.

 Preserve their memories.

 Create a family album, going back as many generations as you can.

 Write a family history.

 Share your family stories with your children.

Keep in touch with current events.

 Subscribe to your community newspaper.

 Read more than one newspaper.

 Watch the news on television.

Tune in to more than one channel.

 Listen to talk radio.

 Read a variety of magazines.

 Discern the difference between reporting and editorializing.

Speak up.

 Speak out.

 Write a letter to the editor.

 Write an Op-Ed (Opinion-Editorial) piece.

Call in your opinion to talk radio.

 Email your newscasters.

 Respond to television editorials.

 Celebrate your right to be heard.

# ★ Americans can name:

Agent 86.

Bruce Wayne's secret identity.

The four presidents depicted on Mount Rushmore.

George Jetson's dog.

Archie Bunker's wife.

Charlie's Angels.

All of the Brady Bunch kids.

A talking horse.

The first lunar landing vehicle.

Remember Pearl Harbor.

 Remember the Alamo.

 Remember the *Maine*.

 Remember D-Day.

 Remember all who have served our country in the armed forces.

Thank God for what you have.

 Thank your parents for raising you well.

 Thank a teacher.

 Thank a police officer.

 Thank a fireman or firewoman.

 Thank a medical professional.

Say "Thank You" often and mean it.

 Bring an apple to your teacher.

 Leave a gift for your postman in your mailbox during the holidays.

 Take cookies to your community fire station.

 Take doughnuts to your neighbor-hood police station.

 Treat teachers, firemen, and policemen with respect; they earn it.

Volunteer to be a Big Brother or Big Sister.

 Volunteer in your community.

 Volunteer at a homeless shelter (and not just during the holiday season).

 Volunteer in a soup kitchen.

 Donate clothing.

 Donate blankets.

# ★ Heroic American Generals:

General Robert E. Lee.

General Ulysses S. Grant.

General George Patton.

General Douglas MacArthur.

General Dwight D. Eisenhower.

General Norman Schwarzkopf.

General Colin Powell.

# ★ American Couples:

George & Martha.

Bonnie & Clyde.

JFK & Jackie.

Ricky & Lucy.

Fred & Ginger.

Gable & Lombard.

Garland & Rooney.

Bogart & Bacall.

Taylor & Burton.

Newman & Woodward.

Hepburn & Tracy.

Rhett & Scarlett.

Fred & Wilma.

Lil' Abner & Daisy Mae.

Barbie & Ken.

Sonny & Cher.

Roy Rogers & Dale Evans.

# ★ Play with old-fashioned American toys . . .

Hula with a hula hoop.

Perfect your tricks with a yo-yo.

Make a Slinky roll down the stairs.

Play stoop ball or stick ball with a Pinky ball.

Grow frustrated with a Rubik's Cube.

Play with a Barbie, a Ken, a Matchbox car,
or a G. I. Joe.

Build a model airplane or car.

Build with Lincoln Logs.

Erect with an Erector set.

Rollerblade.

Use the toys with a kid you love.

Or donate your hula hoop, yo-yo, Slinky,
Pinky ball, Rubik's Cube, Barbie, Ken,
Matchbox cars, G. I. Joe, Lincoln Logs, and
Erector set to a shelter for abused women
and children.

Keep your skates, and rollerblade often with
friends.

# Celebrate school spirit:

Cheerleaders.

Pep rallies.

Proms.

Pom-poms.

Homecoming.

Marching bands.

Be a good neighbor.

 Get to know your
neighbors.

 Bring in your neighbor's trash can.

 Bake a cake to welcome a
new neighbor.

Bake a cake to thank an old neighbor.

 Keep an eye on your neighbor's house while he or she is away.

 Offer to collect your neighbors' mail and newspapers while they're away.

# Quintessentially American:

Diners.

Mickey Mouse.

Elvis Presley.

The Super Bowl.

Cracker Jacks.

Basketball.

Coca-Cola.

Norman Rockwell.

The Lone Ranger.

Milk shakes.

Drive-in movies.

M&M's.

Westerns.

⭐ Help a farmer plow a field.

⭐ Help a farmer harvest a field.

⭐ Milk a cow.

⭐ Slop pigs.

⭐ Collect freshly-laid eggs.

⭐ Muck a barn.

⭐ Appreciate all that America's farmers do to feed us and the world.

 Drive less.

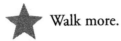 Walk more.

 Carpool.

 Use mass transit.

 Conserve.

Appreciate the foresight, intelligence, and commitment of our Founding Fathers.

 Visit the National Archives.

 View the Constitution, signed by our forefathers.

 Memorize the Preamble to the Constitution.

*We the people of the United States in order to form a more perfect Union, establish Justice, insure domestic Tranquillity, provide for the common defence, promote the general Welfare and secure the Blessings of Liberty to ourselves and our Posterity, do ordain and establish this CONSTITUTION of the United States of America.*

# ★ Memorize the Bill of Rights

**(the first 10 Amendments to the U.S. Constitution)**

These rights include: freedom of speech, freedom of the press, freedom of religion, protection from unreasonable search and seizure, the right to bear arms, and protection under due process of law.

Know the significance of Thomas Paine's *Common Sense*.

*RESOLVED: That these United Colonies are, and of right ought to be, free and independent States, that they are absolved from all allegiance to the British Crown, and that all political connection between them and the State of Great Britain is, and ought to be totally dissolved.*

 Exercise your responsibility to participate in civil disobedience for just causes.

See the Declaration of Independence in the National Archives.

 Have a framed copy of it in your home.

 Memorize the opening of the Declaration of Independence.

*When in the course of human events, it becomes necessary for one people to dissolve the practical bands which have connected them with another, and to assume among the Powers of the earth, the separate and equal situation to which the Laws of Nature and of Nature's God entitle them, a decent respect to the opinions of mankind requires that they should declare the causes which impel them to the separation.*

*We hold these truths to be self evident that all men are created equal, that they are endowed by their Creator with certain unalienable Rights, that among these are Life, Liberty, and*

Understand the *risk* taken by the signatories of the Declaration of Independence.

 Know the significance of the Federalist Papers—and read at least two.

 Read the writings of Abigail Adams.

 Take responsibility—exercise YOUR RIGHT TO VOTE.

# ⭐ Be inspired by some great American words . . .

*"I only regret I have but one life to give for my country."* —Nathan Hale

*"I have not yet begun to fight."* —John Paul Jones

*"Give me liberty or give me death."* —Patrick Henry

*"One if by land, two if by sea."* —Paul Revere

Adopt a child.

 Become a foster parent.

 Adopt a pet from a shelter.

 Host an exchange student.

# ★American heroes:

Amelia Earhart.

Orville and Wilbur Wright.

George Washington.

Jackie Robinson.

John Glenn, Jr.

Neil Armstrong.

John F. Kennedy.

Babe Ruth.

Paul Revere.

Big Bird.

# ⭐ Identify these American phrases:

"Yabba-dabba-doo!"

"Leapin' lizards!"

"Good grief!"

"Nyuk, nyuk, nyuk!"

"Yada, yada, yada."

"Don't have a cow, man."

"Well *excuuuuuuuuuse* me!"

"And awayyyy we go!"

"They're grrrrrreat!"

"Heeecrc's Johnny!"

"Hi-ho, Silver, awaaaay!"

Live with integrity.

 Define your personal principles.

 Stand up for your principles.

 Take responsibility for your actions.

 Hold others responsible for their actions.

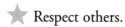 Respect others.

⭐ Respect yourself.

⭐ Be tolerant.

⭐ Be accepting.

⭐ Understand the difference between *tolerating* and *accepting* the beliefs of others.

⭐ Expect the best of others.

⭐ Give the best of yourself.

# Know our American baseball heroes:

Babe Ruth.

Joe DiMaggio.

Ted Williams.

Hank Aaron.

Jackie Robinson.

Mickey Mantle.

Roger Maris.

Mark McGwire.

Sammy Sosa.

Lou Gehrig.

Tony Gwynn.

Barry Bonds.

Cal Ripken.

Yogi Berra.

Nolan Ryan.

Hank Greenberg.

Ernie Banks.

Cy Young.

Reggie Jackson.

# Celebrate an American fad . . .

Pet rocks.

Coonskin caps.

Dance marathons.

Smiley faces.

Pogo sticks.

Mood rings.

Razor Scooters.

# ★ American as A-B-C:

NFL
NHL
MLB
NBA
WNBA
NBC, CBS, ABC, MTV, PBS
WWF
NASCAR
NRA
YMCA
NOW
NAACP
NCAA
NASA

Stop complaining.

 Stop worrying.

 Stop lying.

 Stop eating so much junk food!

Stop rushing.

 Stop swearing, #*@ø*!!

 Stop watching so much TV.

 Stop driving like a maniac.

# Start expanding your horizons . . .

Start doing something constructive.

Start exercising.

Start reading a good book.

Start a new hobby.

Start eating more healthfully.

Start a scrapbook.

Start each day with a smile.

Lower your cholesterol.

 Lower your blood pressure.

 Lower your stress level.

Raise your awareness—meditate.

 Raise your own tomatoes—
plant a garden.

 Raise your I.Q.—read more.

 Raise your kids—with love.

# ⭐ Learn an American dance:

A square dance.

The two-step.

Swing/Jitterbug.

The funky chicken (not to be confused with the "chicken dance").

Disco.

Hand jive.

The hokey-pokey.

The Twist.

The Electric Slide.

The Charleston.

The Virginia Reel.

The Lindy Hop.

Hip-hop.

Express your opinions.

 But don't spread fear.

 Or unconfirmed rumors.

 Listen to opposing opinions.

Have faith.

 Pray.

 Attend a weekly prayer group.

 Practice religious tolerance.

 Read a holy book from a tradition different than your own.

Hug your kids.

 Set a good example for your kids.

 Educate your kids.

 Read a good parenting book. (Or two or three.)

Visit a veteran in a VA hospital.

 Visit a Civil War battlefield.

 Attend a reenactment of a Revolutionary War battle.

 Participate in a reenactment of a Revolutionary War battle.

# ★ One-of-a-kind:

Charlie Chaplin.

Steve Jobs.

Madonna.

Groucho Marx.

Jack Nicholson.

Thomas Jefferson.

Wolfman Jack.

# ⭐ Only in America:

Evel Knievel.

Barney.

Woodstock.

David Letterman's "Top 10" Lists.

Gomer Pyle.

Seeing how many people you can stuff into a phone booth.

Actively maintain your emotional health.

 Actively maintain your spiritual health.

 Actively maintain your physical health.

Pay your taxes.

 Pay your taxes on time.

 Pay your taxes without cheating.

 Pay your taxes without complaining.

Embrace diversity.

 Learn a foreign language.

 Visit different houses of worship within your community.

 Attend a church.

Attend a mosque.

 Attend a temple.

 Attend a synagogue.

 Go out of your way to make foreign visitors feel at home in our country.

Teach an ESL (English as a Second Language) course.

 Mentor an immigrant for the naturalization test.

 Attend an American naturalization ceremony.

 Bring flowers and flags for our new citizens.

Broaden your horizons: Travel to a foreign country.

 Appreciate foreign cultures—and share our culture with them.

 Send postcards to your family and friends.

 When you return home, send postcards from American locations to your foreign friends.

⭐ Watch fireworks on Independence Day.

⭐ Be *careful* with fireworks!

⭐ Teach your children to be careful with fireworks.

⭐ Go on a picnic on Memorial Day.

⭐ Laze on Labor Day.

⭐ Visit a forest preserve on Arbor Day.

⭐ Watch football on Thanksgiving Day. (And eat turkey, too.)

# Work at keeping your family strong. . .

Set aside time for family meals.

Set aside time for family outings.

Set aside time for family discussions.

Set aside time to spend with your other half.

And remember to set aside time to spend with yourself.

Carve a pumpkin on Halloween.

 Help a child carve a pumpkin on Halloween.

 Dress up in costume to give out treats.

 Dress up in costume to go trick-or-treating with your children.

 Decorate your porch for Halloween.

 Create a neighborhood haunted house.

# Parent your children . . .

Talk to them.

Listen to them.

Discipline them.

Teach your kids about kindness.

Teach your kids about responsibility.

Teach your kids about respect.

Teach by example.

Be caring enough to talk with your kids about drugs.

Be brave enough to discuss sex with them.

Accept responsibility for yourself and your family.

Have your kids draw an American flag.

 Frame it and hang it with pride.

 Have them draw the Statue of Liberty, too.

 And the Liberty Bell.

 And an eagle.

# ★ Identify these phrases:

"Follow the Yellow Brick Road."

"May the Force be with you."

"I like Ike."

"Who shot J.R.?"

"Here I come to save the day!"

"Car 54, where are you?"

# Celebrate American holidays . . .

Read Martin Luther King's "I have a dream" speech on Martin Luther King Day.

Watch for Punxsatawney Phil on Groundhog Day.

Watch the movie "Groundhog Day," starring Bill Murray.

Be romantic on Valentine's Day—find great ideas in *1001 Ways To Be Romantic*.

On Presidents Day reflect on what made Washington, Lincoln, and so many of our other presidents great.

Plant a tree on Arbor Day.

Visit a military cemetery or a Veterans Hospital on Veterans Day—and throughout the year.

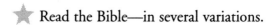 Read the Bible—in several variations.

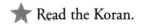 Read the Koran.

⭐ Read the Torah.

⭐ Read the I Ching.

⭐ Read the teachings of Buddha.

⭐ Learn about the religious
holidays of other faiths.

⭐ Live ecumenically.

# ⭐ Identify these phrases:

"Dewey Defeats Truman."

"Just the facts, ma'am."

"Sock it to me."

"All the news that's fit to print."

"Only the Shadow knows!"

"Get your stinking paws off me, you damned, dirty ape!"

"Why don't you come up and see me some time?"

# ★ Be involved in your children's school . ..

Be a class parent.

Chaperone a field trip.

Chaperone a school dance.

Attend Homecoming.

Participate in fundraisers.

Contribute to class parties.

Join the Parent Teacher Association (PTA).

Attend parent/teacher nights.

Attend the school's programs.

Get to know the faculty and the staff.

Encourage your children to do their best.

Show pride in your child's work.

Swim in the Atlantic.

 Swim in the Pacific.

 Swim in the Gulf.

Stand on the shores of each of the Great Lakes.

 Know the names of each of the Great Lakes.

 Learn about the Erie Canal.

Visit the Florida Keys.

 Visit Disney World.

 Hug Mickey Mouse.

Work hard.

 Play hard.

 Keep balance in your life.

Celebrate the beauty of the American terrain.

 Celebrate the Atlantic sunrise.

 Savor a Pacific sunset.

 See spring thaw a Minnesota lake.

Watch the waves break in Bangor, Maine.

 Observe the wildlife in the Florida Everglades.

 Smell the Emerald Forest on the Olympic Peninsula.

 Watch the Blue Angels fly over the blue skies of San Diego.

Tour Hearst Castle in California.

 Attend a chili cook-off in Texas.

 Experience Graceland in Memphis.

 Go to the races in Saratoga.

Make music in Nashville.

 Learn to ski in Idaho.

 Experience cherry blossom time in Washington, D.C.

 Tap a maple tree for syrup in Vermont.

# Close your eyes and see these great American images:

A cowboy riding the range.

The Wright Brothers' first airplane in flight.

A classic Model-T automobile.

Rosie the Riveter.

The Democratic donkey.

The Republican elephant.

Pick apples in October in New York.

 Pick apples in October in Washington.

 Attend an apple festival.

 Bake a fresh apple pie.

Camp in Yosemite.

 Camp in Kings Canyon.

 Raft the American River.

 Pan for gold nears Sutter's Mill.

Take a steamboat ride on the Mississippi River.

 Eat Creole food in New Orleans.

 Listen to blues in New Orleans.

 Visit a New Orleans cemetery.

# ★ Americans who like to scare us:

Edgar Allan Poe.

Stephen King.

R.L. Stine.

John Carpenter.

Wes Craven.

Vincent Price.

Dean Koontz.

V.C. Andrews.

Rod Serling.

# Listen to some songs to get you thinking:

"Abraham, Martin & John," by Dion.

"American Pie," by Don McLean.

"Bridge Over Troubled Water," by Simon & Garfunkel.

"Blowin' in the Wind," by Bob Dylan.

 # Party on!

Tupperware parties.

Frat parties.

Dance parties.

Birthday parties.

Political parties.

Attend a national political convention.

Participate in a national political convention—as a delegate!

⭐ Make the time for a traditional honeymoon.

⭐ Make the time for a second honeymoon.

⭐ Make the time for a third and fourth.

⭐ Honeymoon in the Poconos.

⭐ Honeymoon in Vegas.

⭐ Honeymoon at Niagara Falls.

⭐ Honeymoon in Virginia Beach.

⭐ Honeymoon in Hawaii.

Drive courteously.

 Use your turn signals.

 Let someone change lanes in front of you.

 Use your horn, but only in emergencies.

 Keep your temper.

 Don't fall prey to road rage.

# ⭐ **Identify these phrases:**

"Welcome to Fantasy Island!"

"One of these days, Alice…POW! ZOOM! To the moon!"

"That's one small step for man; one giant leap for mankind."

"The times, they are a-changin'."

"Oh, no—Mister Bill!"

"And now you know…the rest of the story."

"I'm mad as hell and I'm not going to take it anymore!!"

"Smile! You're on Candid Camera!"

Every day, tell those you love that you love them.

 Call your parents.

 Keep in touch with your siblings.

 Visit your grandparents.

 Play with your kids.

 Kiss your spouse.

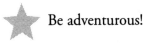 Be adventurous!

 Go for the gusto!

 Take risks!

 Innovate!

# ★America, where bigger is better:

The Grand Canyon.

Wal-Mart.

Microsoft.

"From sea to shining sea."

*Moby Dick.*

SUVs.

The Mississippi River.

# ★ America, where small is beautiful:

Rhode Island.

Palm Pilots.

PCs.

Mobile telephones.

State flowers.

# Cook and eat American foods . . .

Learn to make fried chicken.

Try a Key Lime pie.

Eat a Georgia peach.

Bake a peach cobbler.

Make an apple crisp.

Indulge in potato chips and root beer.

Barbecue hot dogs and hamburgers.

Top them off with potato salad and cole slaw.

Don't forget the ribs.

Garnish with pickles, mustard, ketchup, and relish.

Finish with blueberry turnovers and ice cream.

Or build a banana split, a hot fudge sundae, a root beer float.

Invite a friend to celebrate being American while enjoying all of the above.

# Explore America . . .

Take a trip by train.

Take a trip by bus.

Take your family on an old fashioned driving vacation.

Plant your own garden.

 Help plant a community garden.

 Help plant the seeds of community on a local level.

 Help plant the seeds of community on a national level.

# Americans are:

Honorable.

Loyal.

Tolerant.

Industrious.

Participatory.

Action-oriented.

Practical.

Charitable.

Flexible.

Generous.

Friendly.

Persevering.

Know the philosophies of the Republican, Democratic, Libertarian, and Green parties.

 Volunteer to register voters.

 Volunteer to work the polls.

 Celebrate your right to vote.

# Americans value:

Freedom.

Family.

Individuality.

Creativity.

Growth.

Change.

Inclusion.

Education.

Innovation.

Discovery.

Speed.

# ⭐ Sing some songs with "U.S.A." in their title:

"Surfin' U.S.A.," by the Beach Boys.

"U.S.A. Today," by Hank Williams, Jr.

"R-O-C-K in the U.S.A.," by John Cougar Mellencamp.

"Mister Touchdown U.S.A.," by the University of Michigan Band.

"Back in the U.S.A.," by Chuck Berry.

"Better in the U.S.A," by Glenn Frey.

# Get to know some American personalities:

W.C. Fields.

Bugs Bunny.

Little Richard.

Jay Gatsby.

Truman Capote.

The Fonz.

Michael Jackson.

Joan Rivers.

Attend a rodeo.

 Ride a mechanical bull.

 Learn to twirl a lariat.

 Learn to ride a horse.

# Watch American children's programming with your kids:

*Sesame Street.*

*The Howdy Doody Show.*

*The Electric Company.*

*Captain Kangaroo.*

*Bozo.*

*Pee Wee's Playhouse.*

*Romper Room.*

*Mr. Rogers' Neighborhood.*

*The Mickey Mouse Club.*

# ★ "All American" songs:

"All American," by Sammy Davis, Jr.

"All American Boy," by the Statler Brothers.

"All American Girl," by Melissa Etheridge.

"All American Man," by Kiss.

"All American Redneck," by the Geezinslaw Brothers.

Complain less.

 Solve more.

 Keep humor in your life.

 Accentuate the positive.

 De-emphasize the negative.

 Consider your cup of life as being half full rather than half empty.

Join the Armed Forces.

 Join the Reserves.

 Understand the reasons we help other nations.

 Understand the reasons we support human rights throughout the world.

 Work diligently for peace.

 But be willing to fight.

# ★ Know some American inventors:

Thomas Edison.

Eli Whitney.

Henry Ford.

John Crapper.

Jonas Salk.

Isaac Merritt Singer.

Samuel Morse.

Ray Kurtzweil.

# Know some American originals:

Andy Warhol.

Bob Dylan.

Jackson Pollock.

Abigail van Buren & Ann Landers.

Will Rogers.

Arlo Guthrie.

# ⭐ Know some American legends:

Paul Bunyan.

Louis Armstrong.

Billy the Kid.

Billie Holiday.

Casey Jones.

# ★ Know some American trailblazers:

Lewis and Clark.

Oprah Winfrey.

Johnny Appleseed.

Alan B. Shepard.

Martin Luther King, Jr.

Gloria Steinem.

Susan B. Anthony.

Florence Nightingale.

Read the Sunday comics with your children.

 Help your child build a soapbox racer.

 Read to your children.

 Read *with* your children.

Celebrate family traditions.

 Collect family recipes.

 Host a family reunion.

 Go home for the holidays.

Send an underprivileged kid to summer camp.

 Support a local scholarship fund.

 Volunteer to read to children at your local library.

 Volunteer as a tutor at your local elementary or high school.

Get involved with your community.

 Join your local community organization (Town Council, Planning Group, etc.).

 Support your local community theatre.

 Support your local symphony.

 Support local arts programs.

Hike the Pacific Crest Trail.

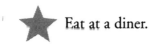 Eat at a diner.

 Get ice cream from an ice cream truck.

 Ride a roller coaster.

 Ride a merry-go-round.

 Ride a go-cart.

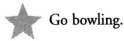 Go bowling.

 Play horseshoes.

 Play spin-the-bottle.

 Play your old LP's.

# Make continuous positive changes in your life:

Exercise your body—move!

Exercise your mind—read a book.

Exercise your heart—help a friend.

Exercise your heart more—help a stranger.

# ★ Being American means:

Being an individual.

Being a team player.

Bringing the best of both to whatever you do.

Be patriotic only on days that end with "Y".

 When you ask someone, "How are you?" *really listen* to their response.

 Understand why America is called the "Melting Pot," and celebrate that it is!

 Hang a framed copy of the Bill of Rights in your home.

# Learn what patriotism means to others . . .

*"Patriotism is proud of a country's virtues and eager to correct its deficiencies."* —Sydney J. Harris

*"Patriotism is a lively sense of collective responsibility."* —Richard Aldington

*"Dissent, rebellion, and all-around hell-raising remain the true duty of patriots."* — Barbara Ehrenreich

*"Patriotism is when love of your own people comes first; nationalism, when hate for other people comes first."* —Charles de Gaulle

**Define what patriotism means to you.**

# ★ America from A to Z

**A** is for America, attitude, Air Force, Army.

**B** is for Bill of Rights, baseball, bounty, Baby Boomers.

**C** is for Constitution, Congress, courts, Coca-Cola, capitalism, colleges.

**D** is for dignity, Democrats, due process of law, Dad, debates.

**E** is for equality, entrepreneur, ecology, education, eagles, elections.

**F** is for flag, freedom, free speech, free press, fireworks.

**G** is for goodness, greatness, gratefulness, giving, growth.

**H** is for happiness, helpfulness, honor, hope.

**I** is for independence, innovation, immigrants, inclusion.

**J** is for justice, joy, jelly beans, Jefferson, jury.

**K** is for Kilroy, kids, Kennebunkport, Kodak.

**L** is for liberty, laws, Labor Day, legislation.

**M** is for Memorial Day, money, Marines, McDonald's, Mom.

**N** is for Navy, nature, New York City.

**O** is for openness, Old Glory, Old Faithful.

**P** is for peace, prosperity, Polaroid, patriotism, privacy.

**Q** is for Quakers, quiet strength, *quid pro quo*, quill.

**R** is for research, reason, rights, Republicans, Rosie the Riveter.

**S** is for states, Sousa marches, sharing, Statue of Liberty, salute.

**T** is for Thanksgiving, tolerance, Texas Rangers, teepees.

**U** is for Uncle Sam, United States of America, universal suffrage, universities.

**V** is for voting, veterans, Viagra, vigor.

**W** is for Washington, D.C., worship, winners, Winnebagos, wild turkey.

**X** is for the eXtra hand you lend someone in need.

**Y** is for yes, yearbooks, yuppie, Yoo Hoo, youth, "yippie-yi-o-ki-ay."

**Z** is for zeal, zest, zoos, ZIP Codes.

# Watch a bigger-than-life hero on the big screen:

Sylvester Stallone in *Rocky*.

Arnold Schwarzenegger in *Terminator 2*.

Bruce Willis in *Die Hard*.

Charlton Heston in *The Ten Commandments*.

Harrison Ford in *Raiders of the Lost Ark*.

# ★ Know our American tennis heroes:

Arthur Ashe.

Jimmy Connors.

Martina Navratilova.

Billie Jean King.

Chris Evert.

Steffi Graf.

Monica Seles.

Venus and Serena Williams.

John McEnroe.

Andre Agassi.

Pete Sampras.

Jennifer Capriati.

Share a Happy Meal with your kid for lunch.

 Share a Hershey Bar for dessert.

 Visit the Hershey factory in Hershey, Pennsylvania.

 Then go to Hershey Park.

Go to a county fair.

 Go to a state fair.

 Watch the Rose Bowl Parade.

 Watch the Macy's
Thanksgiving Day Parade.

 March in a parade in your own
community.

# How many great American couples can you name?

Ozzie & Harriet.

Porgy & Bess.

Blondie & Dagwood.

Archie & Edith.

Archie & Veronica.

Boris & Natasha.

Burns & Allen.

Clark & Lois.

Kermit & Miss Piggy.

Mickey & Minnie.

Mork & Mindy.

Nancy & Sluggo.

# Did you know that songs titled "America" were recorded by:

Simon & Garfunkel.

Neil Diamond.

Pat Boone.

Prince.

Heart.

Waylon Jennings.

⭐ Be environmentally aware.

⭐ Speak out on important environmental issues.

⭐ Participate in beach and park clean-ups.

⭐ Use environmentally safe pest control.

⭐ Recycle.

⭐ Pick up a piece of trash.

⭐ Do your part to keep America beautiful and environmentally safe.

Help a stranger change a flat tire.

 Offer your cell phone to someone stuck on the highway.

 Don't slow down to stare at accidents.

 Say a prayer instead.

Bring a positive attitude to the workplace.

 Keep that positive attitude no matter how it is challenged.

 Maintain your sense of humor in spite of stress.

 Share your positive attitude and sense of humor with others.

 View your coworkers as your 9-to-5 family and treat them as such.

# Know your American trivia:

Name the people pictured on our paper money:

$1—George Washington.

$2—Thomas Jefferson.

$5—Abraham Lincoln.

$10— Alexander Hamilton.

$20—Andrew Jackson.

$50—Ulysses S. Grant.

$100—Benjamin Franklin.

**Name the Andrews Sisters:**

Maxine.
Laverne.
Patty.

**Name the thirteen original American colonies.**

Virginia
New York
Massachusetts
New Hampshire
Maryland
Connecticut
Rhode Island
Delaware
North Carolina
New Jersey
South Carolina
Pennsylvania
Georgia

Visit Mt. Vernon.

 Visit Monticello.

 Visit Kitty Hawk, North Carolina.

 Visit Pearl Harbor.

 Visit Ford's Theatre.

# Marvel at these American brains:

Henry David Thoreau.

Ralph Waldo Emerson.

Buckminster Fuller.

Richard Feynman.

Benjamin Franklin.

Albert Einstein (naturalized American).

Booker T. Washington.

# Laugh along with Americans who have made us laugh:

Lucille Ball.

Groucho, Harpo, Chico (and Gummo and Zeppo) Marx.

Buster Keaton.

Jerry Lewis.

Jack Benny.

Jonathan Winters.

Robin Williams.

Andy Rooney.

Bill Cosby.

Mel Brooks.

# Read the works of American poets who inspire us:

Emily Dickinson.

Walt Whitman.

Robert Frost.

e.e. cummings.

Ralph Waldo Emerson.

Jack Kerouac.

T.S. Eliot.

Ezra Pound.

Carl Sandburg.

Maya Angelou.

# Appreciate Americans who have entertained us:

Bob Hope.

Johnny Carson.

Frank Sinatra.

Glenn Miller.

Nat King Cole.

Sammy Davis, Jr.

Walt Disney.

Steven Spielberg.

Stephen King.

Billy Crystal.

David Letterman.

Jay Leno.

# Know our American Olympic heroes:

Scott Hamilton.

Mary Lou Retton.

The 1988 U.S. Hockey Team.

Wilma Rudolph.

Carl Lewis.

Basketball "Dream Teams."

Florence Griffith Joyner.

Greg Louganis.

Jackie Joyner-Kersee.

Tara Lipinski.

Jim Thorpe.

Peggy Fleming.

Mark Spitz.

Play baseball.

 Teach your kids to play baseball.

 Go to a ball game.

 Take your kids to a ball game.

 Sing along to "Take Me Out to the Ball Game."

 Eat lots of peanuts and Cracker Jack and a stadium dog or two.

Value life.

 Know your blood type.

 Be a blood donor.

 Be an organ donor.

 Drive sober.

# ★ Ship-Shape America:

*Niña, Pinta,* and *Santa Maria.*

The *Mayflower.*

U.S.S. *Enterprise.*

The *Pequod.*

U.S.S. *Pueblo.*

U.S.S. *Constitution* ("Old Ironsides.")

U.S.S. *Nautilus.*

Read a history book.

 Watch the History Channel.

 Take a history course.

 Discuss history with friends.

 Remember that those who forget history are bound to repeat it.

Learn about Native American cultures.

 Honor them.

 Honor America's heritage.

 Honor your family's heritage.

# Sing some classically patriotic songs:

"America the Beautiful."

"I'm a Yankee Doodle Dandy."

"My Country 'Tis of Thee."

"You're a Grand Old Flag."

"God Bless America."

# ★ Marvelous, mythical USA places:

Dogpatch.

Lake Wobegon.

Hooterville.

Mudville.

Knot's Landing.

Mayberry.

The Ponderosa.

Gotham City.

Metropolis.

Yoknapatawpha County.

Make time to enjoy yourself, your
family, and others you care for.

 Never let a day go by without doing something totally
selfless.

 Never let a day go by without doing
something totally for yourself.

 See the promise and
opportunity in every day.

Respect those in service industries.

 Value the services they provide.

 When possible, address them by name.

 Tip well for good service.

# ⭐ Up, up and away!

*Mercury.*

*Gemini.*

*Apollo.*

The Hubble telescope.

The space shuttle.

The robotic Mars explorer.

*Voyager.*

Go to Coney Island for hot
dogs and ice cream.

 Ride the roller coaster
while you're there.

# ★ American brothers & sisters

The Marx Brothers.

The Lennon Sisters.

The Andrews Sisters.

The Blues Brothers.

Warner Bros.

The Wright Brothers.

Brooks Brothers.

The Smothers Brothers.

# ★ Great American Broadway musicals:

*Oklahoma!*

*West Side Story.*

*Hair.*

*The Producers.*

*Rent.*

*Grease.*

*South Pacific.*

*1776.*

*Bye Bye Birdie.*

Decorate cookies with red, white and blue sprinkles.

 Make a "flag cake" using red, white and blue frosting.

 Serve patriotic cupcakes: Top them with tiny American flags.

 Serve Campbell's Tomato Soup to your family.

 Give your kids red, white and blue Gummy Bears.

# Americans . . .

…can explain the Infield Fly Rule.

…can sing the theme song to "The Brady Bunch."

…know who said: "What you see is what you get!"

…can sing the theme song to "Gilligan's Island."

# ★ Patriotic ideas from A to Z:

**Appreciate** America.

**Be** there when you're needed.

**Count** your blessings.

**Do** your duty.

**Enjoy** freedom.

**Fight** for freedom.

**Give** of yourself.

**Honor** the flag.

**Invent** new ways of doing things.

**Join** a volunteer organization.

**Keep** on truckin'.

**Love** it or leave it.

**Make** things better.

**Negotiate** peaceful resolutions.

**Open** your arms, your heart and your mind.

**Pull** your own weight.

**Question** authority.

**Recite** the Pledge of Allegiance proudly.

**Sing** "The Star Spangled Banner."

**Teach** tolerance.

**Understand** others.

**Vote** in local, state and national elections.

**Work** to keep America great.

**Xtend** yourself for others.

**Yup!** We celebrate being American!

**Zero** in on what's really important.

**Value peace, work for peace . . .
but not at all costs.**

*"Peace can endure only so long as humanity
really insists upon it, and is willing to work
for it and sacrifice for it."*
—Franklin D. Roosevelt

"*It must be a peace without victory. Victory would mean peace forced upon the losers, a victor's terms imposed upon the vanquished.*"
—Woodrow Wilson

"*Peace, commerce and honest friendship with all nations; entangling alliances with none.*"
—Thomas Jefferson

"*Let there be peace on earth / And let it begin with me.*"

—Hymn by Sy Miller

"*You can't separate peace from freedom because no one can be at peace unless he has his freedom.*"

—Malcolm X

*"If peace cannot be maintained with honour, it is no longer peace."*

—John Russell

**Work for peace in your own life in your own way.**

# ★ Listen to a medley of America-related songs:

"American Tune," by Paul Simon.

"Fourth of July," by Dave Alvin.

"Here Comes the Freedom Train," by Merle Haggard.

"House I Live In (That's America to Me)," by Frank Sinatra.

"I Am a Patriot," by Jackson Browne.

"Independence Day," by Bruce Springsteen.

Write a love letter to your husband or wife.

 Write a keepsake letter to your young child.

 Write "thank you" letters.

 Make a family time capsule.

# Great American buddies and teams:

Rocky & Bullwinkle.

Laverne & Shirley.

Starsky & Hutch.

Beavis & Butthead.

Felix & Oscar.

Mary & Rhoda.

Lucy & Ethel.

Calvin & Hobbes.

Tom & Jerry.

Bert & Ernie.

Amos & Andy.

Laurel & Hardy.

The Lone Ranger & Tonto.

Batman & Robin.

Simon & Garfunkel.

Jan & Dean.

Butch Cassidy & The Sundance Kid.

Martin & Lewis.

Cagney & Lacey.

Rowan & Martin.

Cheech & Chong.

Penn & Teller.

Diana Ross & The Supremes.

Smokey Robinson & The Miracles.

Gladys Night & The Pips

Tom Petty & The Heartbreakers.

Huntley & Brinkley.

Lewis & Clark.

Mutt & Jeff.

Rodgers & Hammerstein.

# Appreciate
# your buddies
# and pals.

Sing in the shower.

 Dance at weddings.

 Whistle while you work.

 Tell a good story.

 Tell a joke (suitable for a kid to hear).

# At least once in your life, drive an American muscle car:

Mustang.

Camaro.

GTO.

Thunderbird.

Shelby Cobra.

Corvette.

# ★ Know our American track & field heroes:

Jackie Joyner-Kersee.

Carl Lewis.

Jesse Owens.

Bruce Jenner.

Jim Thorpe.

Wilma Rudolph.

Florence Griffith Joyner.

# Know our American golf heroes:

Bobby Jones.

Jack Nicklaus.

Arnold Palmer.

Lee Trevino.

Ben Hogan.

Tiger Woods.

# Remember the corner candy store?

**Introduce a child to:**

Pez.

Necco wafers.

Pixy Stix.

Wax lips.

Taffy.

Nerds.

Pop Rocks.

Candy Dips.

Sugar Babies.

Tootsie Rolls.

Mike & Ikes.

Bottle Caps.

Fruit Stripe gum.

Chiclets.

Mary Janes.

Charleston Chews.

Bit-O-Honey.

Now & Later.

Cornnuts.

Dots.

Candy necklace.

M&M's.

Rocket pops.

Red Hots.

Fireballs.

Juicy Fruit gum.

Doublemint gum.

Hubba-Bubba bubblegum.

Bazooka Joe bubblegum.

Lifesavers.

# "See the U.S.A. in your Cheverolet . . ."

Visit the Great Smoky Mountains.

Hike in the Painted Desert.

Enjoy the autumn leaves in New England.

Camp in Yellowstone Park.

Travel back through history in Colonial Williamsburg.

Sail on Lake George.

Explore Howe Caverns.

Ride the "Maid of the Mist" under Niagara Falls.

Take a bite out of the Big Apple.

Discover Bryce Canyon.

Raft the Colorado River.

# ⭐ An American mind is an open mind:

**Read a controversial tract:**

Read *Common Sense*, by Thomas Paine.

Read *Mein Kampf*, by Adolf Hitler.

Read *Quotations from Chairman Mao Tse-Tung*.

Read *Profiles in Courage*, by John F. Kennedy.

# ★ Celebrate great American films:

Watch *The Patriot*, starring Mel Gibson.

Watch *Dances With Wolves*, starring Kevin Costner.

Watch *Casablanca*, starring Humphrey Bogart and Ingrid Bergman.

Watch *Saving Private Ryan*, starring Tom Hanks.

Watch *The Great Escape*, starring Steve McQueen.

Watch *Patton*, starring George C. Scott.

Plan a hayride.

 Take a child to the circus.

 Participate in a pie-eating contest.

 Host an ice cream social.

 Take your significant other out for dinner and a movie.

# Gone but not forgotten:

**Find someone who remembers and can explain to you...**

Burma Shave.

Five-and-dime stores.

Reingold beer.

Cranks on cars.

Rotary telephones.

The old Sears Roebuck & Co. catalog.

# Know our American basketball heroes:

Michael Jordan.

Larry Bird.

Kareem Abdul-Jabbar.

Phil Jackson.

Shaquille O'Neal.

Magic Johnson.

Julius Erving.

Pat Riley.

Wilt Chamberlain.

# Know our American football heroes:

Joe Montana.

Joe Namath.

Walter Payton.

Jerry Rice.

Vince Lombardi.

Johnny Unitas.

Brett Favre.

John Elway.

Mike Ditka.

Troy Aikman.

Tom Landry.

John Heisman.

Knute Rockne.

# Know our American sports heroes:

Joe Louis.

Muhammad Ali.

Bobby Orr.

Rocky Marciano.

Dale Earnhardt.

Mia Hamm.

George Foreman.

# ★ Get to know some American originals:

Grandma Moses.

Howard Cosell.

James Dean.

Garrison Keillor.

Jacqueline Kennedy Onassis.

Read *Casey at the Bat*, by Ernest Lawrence Thayer.

 Visit the Baseball Hall of Fame Museum in Cooperstown, New York.

 Attend the World Series.

 Attend the All-Star Game.

Climb Mount Washington in New Hampshire (6,288 feet).

 Climb Mount Whitney in California (14,494 feet).

 Climb the Statue of Liberty (354 steps).

 Climb the Washington Monument (896 steps).

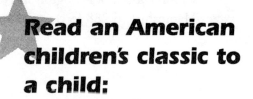

# Read an American children's classic to a child:

*The Cat in the Hat*, by Dr. Seuss.

*The Wizard of Oz*, by L. Frank Baum.

*Charlotte's Web*, by E.B. White.

*The Adventures of Br'er Rabbit*, by Joel Chandler Harris.

The *Little House on the Prairie* series, by Laura Ingalls Wilder.

*Where the Wild Things Are*, by Maurice Sendak.

The *Nancy Drew* series, by Carolyn Keene.

The *Hardy Boys* series, by Franklin Dixon.

*Little Women* and *Little Men*, by Louisa May Alcott.

*Rip Van Winkle*, by Washington Irving.

Support the Boy Scouts and Girl Scouts.

 Support the Campfire Boys & Girls, and the 4-II Club, too.

 Take your kids camping.

 Teach them about Smokey the Bear.

 Make s'mores.

# Dubious achievements:

The Edsel.

Twinkies.

Credit cards.

MTV.

Ride a Harley-Davidson motorcycle.

 Play Bingo.

 Make a quilt.

# ★ Great American quotes to live by:

*"We have nothing to fear but fear itself."*
—Franklin D. Roosevelt

*"If a man hasn't discovered something that he will die for, he isn't fit to live."* —Martin Luther King, Jr.

*"A man is rich according to what he gives, not what he has."* —Henry Ward Beecher

*"I will act as if what I do makes a difference."*
—William James

# Take a bite out of the Big Apple . . .

Celebrate New Year's Eve in Times Square.

Watch the St. Patrick's Day Parade.

Attend a Broadway show.

Visit the Statue of Liberty.

See the Rockettes at Radio City Music Hall.

Go on a **buggy** ride through Central Park.

View New York from the top of the Empire State Building.

**Some of the more meaningful—if not downright inspiring—lyrics from great American songs:**

"Shoo-bop, shoo-bop!"

"Doo-wop, doo-wop, doo-wop!"

"Rama-lama-ding-dong!"

"Ooh-weem-a-way, ooh-weem-a-way."

"Shoo-be, shoo-be, doo!"

*"No arsenal or no weapon in the arsenal of the world is so formidable as the will and moral courage of free men and women."*
—Ronald Reagan

*"Let every nation know, whether it wishes us well or ill, that we shall pay any price, bear any burden, meet any hardship, support any friend, oppose any foe to assure the survival and the success of liberty."*
—John F. Kennedy

Anti-American: Prejudice.

 Anti-American: Intolerance.

 Anti-American: Narrow-mindedness.

 Anti-American: Censorship.

Be a voice against bigotry.

 Be a voice against intolerance.

 Be a voice for acceptance.

 Be a voice for equality.

 Be a person who walks your talk.

# Great words that have inspired Americans:

*"I may disagree with what you say, but I will defend to the death your right to say it."*
—Voltaire

*"No taxation without representation."*
—Thomas Paine

*"Never give in."* —Winston Churchill

Practice what you preach.

 Practice the teachings of your religion.

 Practice the beliefs of your philosophy.

 Practice playing "America the Beautiful" on guitar.

## Some songs to pump you up:

"R-O-C-K in the U.S.A," by John Cougar Mellencamp.

"America," by Neil Diamond.

"Gonna Fly Now," theme song from the movie *Rocky*.

America: Home of the United Nations.

 America: Land of the free and home of the brave.

 America: Home of rock 'n' roll.

 America: Home of the Whopper.

# Here's how some people define America:

*"America is the world's living myth."* —Don DeLillo

*"America is a vast conspiracy to make you happy."* —John Updike

*"America lives in the heart of every man everywhere who wishes to find a region where he will be free to work out his destiny as he chooses."* —Woodrow Wilson

*"America is the civilization of people engaged in transforming themselves."* —Harold Rosenberg

"America is God's Crucible, the great Melting-Pot where all the races of Europe are melting and re-forming!" —Israel Zangwill

"America is a much newer experiment in human living, one with moral concerns at its core." —Yi-Fu Tuan

"America is not anything if it consists of each of us. It is something only if it consists of all of us." —Woodrow Wilson

**How do *you* define America?**

Feel pride.

 Cultivate humility.

 Practice forgiveness.

 Learn compromise.

Foster understanding.

 Count your blessings every day.

 Remember: Those with different opinions are exercising their right to free speech.

*"Ask not what your country can do for you—ask what you can do for your country."*

—John F. Kennedy